CIVICS
Q & A

WHY DO WE PAY TAXES?

Leslie Harper

PowerKiDS
press.
New York

Published in 2013 by The Rosen Publishing Group, Inc.
29 East 21st Street, New York, NY 10010

First Edition

Editor: Jennifer Way
Book Design: Ashley Drago
Layout Design: Andrew Povolny

Photo Credits: Cover, p. 16 Jupiterimages/Workbook Stock/Getty Images; p. 4 TFoxFoto/Shutterstock.com; p. 5 (top) Lawrence Migdale/Stone/Getty Images; p. 5 (bottom) Morgan Lane Photography/Shutterstock.com; p. 6 Deklofenak/Shutterstock.com; p. 8 Roy Hsu/Photographer's Choice RF/Getty Images; p. 9 Fuse/Getty Images; p. 10 Hemera/Thinkstock; p. 11 Jeff Greenberg/Age Fotostock/Getty Images; pp. 12, 15 Jupiterimages/Comstock/Thinkstock; p. 13 Jaimie Duplass/Shutterstock.com; p. 17 Radius Images/Getty Images; p. 18 Kropic1/Shutterstock.com; p. 19 Win McNamee/Getty Images; p. 21 Andersen Ross/Blend Images/Getty Images.

Library of Congress Cataloging-in-Publication Data

Harper, Leslie.
  Why do we pay taxes? / by Leslie Harper. — 1st ed.
    p. cm. — (Civics Q&A)
  Includes index.
  ISBN 978-1-4488-7434-7 (library binding) — ISBN 978-1-4488-7507-8 (pbk.) —
  ISBN 978-1-4488-7581-8 (6-pack)
  1. Taxation—United States. 2. Income tax—United States. 3. Fiscal policy—United States. I. Title.
  HJ2381.H29 2013
  336.200973—dc23
                                    2012000388

Manufactured in the United States of America

CPSIA Compliance Information: Batch #SW12PK: For Further Information contact Rosen Publishing, New York, New York at 1-800-237-9932

CONTENTS

WHAT ARE TAXES?

Firefighters are an important part of keeping the people in a community safe.

Have you ever seen a fire truck coming down the street? Have you ever wondered who buys the fire trucks, pays the firefighters, and builds the roads they drive on?

The money for all of these things comes from **taxes** that people pay to the government. People pay taxes on money they earn and money they spend. The government then uses this money to provide firehouses, post offices, schools, and other important things in a community. This book will teach you about how taxes work and what they pay for.

Taxes help pay people who work in services the government provides, such as the postal service.

A public school is a school that all children in a community can attend. Taxes are used to support public schools.

5

WHAT IS A SALES TAX?

The county or city in which you live may have additional sales tax on top of your state's sales tax.

The next time you are shopping, look at the price of something you plan to buy. When you pay for it, the cost may be higher than what was on the price tag. That extra money you are charged is called a **sales tax**.

The amount that you pay in sales tax is a **percentage** of what an item costs. That means that if the sales tax in your state is 8 percent, you would pay 8¢ in sales tax for every dollar that you spend. The percentage that is charged for a sales tax is decided by each state.

This map of the United States shows the states that have no sales tax. They are Alaska, Delaware, Montana, New Hampshire, and Oregon.

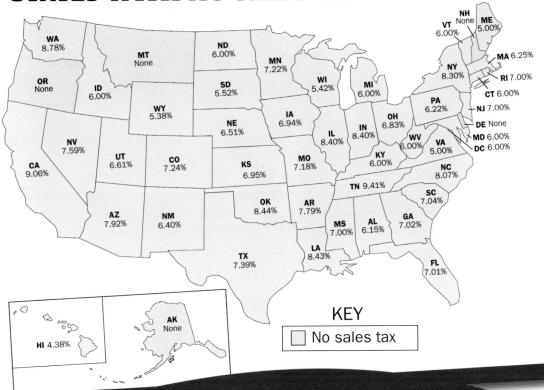

STATES WITH NO SALES TAX

WA 8.78%
OR None
MT None
ND 6.00%
MN 7.22%
ID 6.00%
SD 5.52%
WI 5.42%
MI 6.00%
NH None
VT 6.00%
ME 5.00%
NY 8.30%
MA 6.25%
RI 7.00%
CT 6.00%
NV 7.59%
WY 5.38%
NE 6.51%
IA 6.94%
IL 8.40%
IN 8.40%
OH 6.83%
PA 6.22%
NJ 7.00%
DE None
CA 9.06%
UT 6.61%
CO 7.24%
KS 6.95%
MO 7.18%
KY 6.00%
WV 6.00%
VA 5.00%
MD 6.00%
DC 6.00%
AZ 7.92%
NM 6.40%
OK 8.44%
AR 7.79%
TN 9.41%
NC 8.07%
SC 7.04%
MS 7.00%
AL 6.15%
GA 7.02%
TX 7.39%
LA 8.43%
FL 7.01%

HI 4.38%
AK None

KEY
☐ No sales tax

WHAT ARE PROPERTY TAXES?

Police officers serve their community. The police are a service that is supported by local taxes such as property taxes.

If your parents own a house, they likely pay a **property tax** each year. City and county governments collect property taxes. The local government uses this money to pay for services the community needs, such as public schools.

To decide how much someone will pay in property taxes, a **tax assessor** must first decide how much a property is worth. This person looks at where the property is located, what improvements have been made to the property, and the value of nearby properties. The property tax owed is a percentage of what the property is worth.

Homeowners are not the only people who pay property taxes. People who own apartment buildings or buildings for businesses pay property taxes, too.

WHAT ARE INCOME TAXES?

If a person's income tax is not taken from his paycheck, he must send income tax payments to the IRS.

An **income tax** is based on how much money a person earns each year. Generally, the more money people earn, the more income tax they pay. The **federal** government, as well as many state and local governments, collects income taxes. Income tax is usually taken out of a person's paycheck.

Once a year, people file their taxes with the **Internal Revenue Service**, or IRS, to make sure they have paid the correct amount. If they have paid too little, they will owe money to the government. If they have paid too much, the government gives them **refunds**.

The main office of the IRS is in Washington, D.C. There are smaller offices located throughout the United States, though.

UNITED STATES

Internal Revenue Service Building

WHAT DO LOCAL TAXES PAY FOR?

Local taxes are taxes paid to a city or county government. Most of this money comes from property taxes. First, members of the local government decide how much money they will need to spend in a year. Then they decide how much property owners must pay in taxes.

Local taxes are used to build, maintain, and clean the parks in your city.

It is easy to look around and see local taxes in action. Local governments use tax money to pay for things that we use every day, such as public schools, hospitals, and libraries, as well as garbage pickup. Local taxes even help keep roads safe and local parks beautiful!

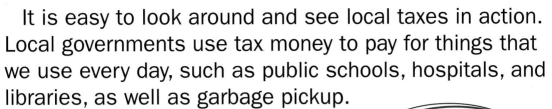

The books you check out of a library were bought using money from local taxes.

WHAT DO STATE TAXES PAY FOR?

State governments get much of their money from state income taxes and sales taxes. States then use this money for many of the things that keep their cities and towns running. On average, states spend about one-quarter of their money on public education. The money is given to local governments, which use it to build schools, buy supplies, and pay teachers.

State taxes also pay for public colleges and universities and state parks. The money from state taxes is used to build and fix roads. It also provides for state police, who patrol roads to keep people from breaking traffic laws.

Each state has at least one public college. The tax money that supports state colleges helps bring down the fees students pay to attend.

WHAT DO FEDERAL TAXES PAY FOR?

Federal taxes pay members of the military. The military includes the Army, Navy, Air Force, Marine Corps, and Coast Guard.

Federal taxes pay for things that keep the entire country safe and running. The federal government spends about 60 percent of its money on three important areas. The first is national **security**. Tax money pays for the US military.

The second area is Social Security, a program that provides money to people who have retired or cannot work.

The last major area of spending is health care. This tax money goes to programs that provide health care to people who are **elderly**, disabled, or very poor.

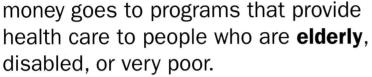

Federal taxes pay for Medicare, which provides health care to the elderly. These taxes also fund Medicaid, which is health care for the poor or disabled.

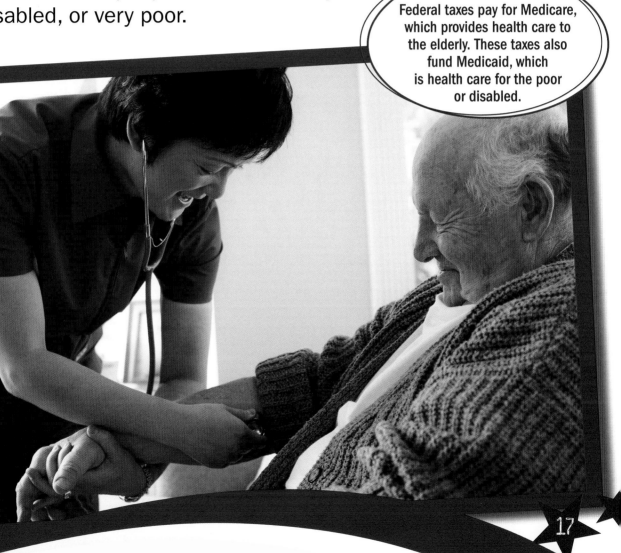

Congress meets in the Capitol, in Washington, D.C.

The federal government is divided into three branches. These branches share power and have different jobs. The branch that makes laws is called the **legislative branch**. It is made up of a group called Congress.

18

Members of Congress write and pass laws about many things, including federal taxes. The US Constitution gives them this power. Congress decides what types of taxes people will pay. It also decides how much each tax will be. The IRS then collects the tax money. The IRS is part of another branch of government, called the executive branch.

The Constitution, shown here, states that Congress has the power to create and collect taxes.

Congress is made up of members of both the House of Representatives and the Senate. This picture shows a meeting of both parts of Congress.

19

Some people do not like paying taxes. They think it is unfair that they must give money that they have earned to the government. However, taxes pay for things that we all need and use. Without taxes, schools, libraries, and parks would not be free and open to everyone. There would be no money to build roads and bridges.

Taxes are an important part of our society. Not everyone will use every service that taxes pay for. However, we can think of these services as safety nets. If we ever need them, they will be there!

Everyone benefits from at least some of the things taxes pay for. Taxes help keep our communities running smoothly and safely.

TAXES Q&A

1

Q: What was the first public library paid for by taxes in the United States?

A: Many people agree that the Peterborough Town Library in New Hampshire was the first public library paid for with tax money. It opened in 1833.

2

Q: How many public schools are in the United States?

A: The United States has nearly 100,000 public schools!

3

Q: What other things do federal taxes pay for?

A: Federal tax money pays for many things, such as food stamps, affordable housing programs, and benefits for veterans, or people who have served in the military.

4

Q: Which public university has the most students?

A: Arizona State University has the most students. More than 58,000 students went there in the 2010 to 2011 school year.

5

Q: Are there any things that we buy that we do not pay a sales tax on?

A: Many states do not charge a sales tax on food from a grocery store or medicines that a doctor tells you to take.

6

Q: How many state parks are there in the United States?

A: There are 6,624 state parks. More than 700 million people visit these parks every year!

GLOSSARY

elderly (EL-der-lee) Older than middle age.

federal (FEH-duh-rul) Having to do with the central government.

income tax (IN-kum TAKS) A tax on the amount of money a person or business makes.

Internal Revenue Service (in-TUR-nel REH-veh-noo SIR-vis) The part of the US government that collects federal taxes.

legislative branch (LEH-jis-lay-tiv BRANCH) The part of the government that makes laws.

percentage (per-SEN-tij) One part of 100.

property tax (PRO-per-tee TAKS) A tax charged on land or buildings that people own.

refunds (REE-fundz) Money that is returned.

sales tax (SAYLZ TAKS) A tax charged on certain things people buy.

security (sih-KYUR-ih-tee) Safety or freedom from danger.

tax assessor (TAKS uh-SEH-sur) A person who decides how much a property is worth.

taxes (TAKS-ez) Money added to the price of something or paid to a government for community services.

INDEX

WEBSITES

Due to the changing nature of Internet links, PowerKids Press has developed an online list of websites related to the subject of this book. This site is updated regularly. Please use this link to access the list:
www.powerkidslinks.com/civ/tax/